The Apple Tree
Voices from School

Don Wagner

First Edition
Copyright ©2005

All Rights Reserved

Published in the United States of America

High Way Publishing
P.O. Box 160
Lecompton, KS 66050

Printed by Memories Bound, Inc./Salina, Kansas
Publishing Consultant: Derius Mammen

ISBN 0-9747220-0-6

Printed in the United States of America

The Apple Tree
Voices from School

<u>D</u> Bar Press
Bennington, Kansas 67422

Acknowledgements

I am indebted to:

- The many friends and colleagues who share my love for education.

- The students who wanted to learn—and especially those who didn't know they did.

- The public school system in America—in spite of all its faults, it is still a beautiful concept.

Also by Don Wagner
D̲ Bar Press

Land of Three Rivers
Poems from the Prairies

The Hell Cow (Compact Disc)
Original Songs and Poems

Bringing Home the Bull
Cowboy Poetry

This book is a work of fiction. Any resemblance to persons, living or dead, is purely coincidental.

Table of Contents

The Apple Tree 1
School Building 2
Literature Teacher 3
Honor Student 4
The Whole Role 6
Biology Lesson 7
Food Service 8
Anticipatory Set 9
No Point 10
Labels 11
Music Teacher 12
Another Day 13
Cheerleader 14
Wrong Lesson 15
Copy Machine Repairman 16
Teacher's Lounge 17
Junior High Coach 18
Student Athlete 19
The Gifted Handicap 20
History Teacher 21
It's How You Play the Game 22
Creating The Past 24
In The Closet 25
Research Paper 26
Athletic Director 27
Guitar Star 28
School Secretary 29
The Janitor's Last Day on the Job 30
Official 31
Final Exam 32
Phys Ed Teacher 33
Please Ask 34

Prejudice	36
Government Teacher	37
Counselor	38
The System	40
Old Guard	41
Serving Time in ISS	42
Librarian	44
Substitute Teacher	45
A Teaching Model	46
Fight	48
Not Enough Time	49
Foreign Language Instructor	50
Publications Room	51
Homecoming Queen	52
Runner Up	53
The Alumni	54
Drama Director	55
Football Coach	56
Dropout	58
Science Teacher	59
A Lesson In Ethics	60
Unnatural Selection	62
Snow Day	63
The Dilbert Principal	64
Committees	65
School Bus Driver	66
New Tattoo	68
Shop Teacher	69
Jock	70
Support Group	71
The Wrong Questions	72
Special Ed Teacher	73
All Prejudices Aside	74
Driver's Education	75
Retirement	76

SCHOOL RULES	78
FELLOWSHIP OF CHRISTIAN ATHLETES	79
GYMN FLOOR	80
MATH TEACHER	81
FOOTBALL STADIUM	82
EARLY ENLISTMENT	83
ATTENDANCE OFFICER	84
TEACHER'S KID	85
PRINCIPAL	86
GROUNDS FOR DISMISSAL	88
STUDENT TEACHER	90
QUIET ONES	91
FUNERAL	92
SCHOOL NURSE	93
THE NEW HOME ECONOMICS	94
SUPERINTENDENT	95
AN ART	96
SCHOOL BOARD	97
JANITOR	98
SENIORITIS	100
ALTERED CIRCUMSTANCE	101
DUMB AND DUMBER DUDES	102
WE WANT DISCRETE FOREIGNERS	103
AWARDS ASSEMBLY	104
SCHOLARSHIP	105
EITHER/OR	106
MORNING SCARS	107
KEYNOTE SPEAKER	108
HOLIDAY BLUES	110
LOST SPIRIT	111
ANACHRONISM	112
CREATIONISM VS EVOLUTION	114
IVORY TOWER	115
WHY I TEACH	116
SEMESTER'S END	118

The Apple Tree

The Chinese say that a teacher's life
Is symbolized by an apple tree;
Students are the ripened fruit
By which the tree is known.

Some apples fall prey to worms and wind,
A few to the bite of bird and bat;
Most grow to maturity on the tree,
Rich fruit surrounding seed.

So it is inside the system
Where students ascend the graded paths,
Seeking light to guide their lives,
All possibilities under the sun.

So we labor under laden boughs,
Endeavoring to bring each fruit to harvest;
Knowing not where the end results
Of our efforts will grow anew.

School Building

A building without people
Is just a shell of steel;
A hallway without footsteps
Reflects an empty feel.
It's the faces which give life,
The bodies which make real;
It's the fact that we attend
That gives a school appeal.

Literature Teacher

All my life I've loved to read,
To find the world within the words,
Discover the nuance in the phrase.

I decided to teach that which I love,
Cast literary pearls before my class,
Open pages to my favorite lines.

I've learned since then that not all share
My love for this, the printed word;
The truths, thoughts, stories written down.

But every once in a while I'll see
The light click on in a student's eye
At an understanding of the work,

And I know then that what I love
Will live on beyond my limited reach.
The seed I planted will surely grow

In minds that I have helped to plow.
The beauty of words from ages past
Lives on as long as someone reads.

Honor Student

I am the type of student
Whom others emulate.
My mind is clear and
Focused on my tasks.
Chiron was my teacher
Or others nearly like him;
My mind burns bright
With Apollo's light of day.
Algebraic equations and
Calculinear curves
I can graph and plot in lines
Of mathematical grace;
Searches on the internet
Reveal to me the web
Of the cosmopolitan
World of inner space.
My writings woo the reader
Unto my point of view;
Prose and poetry nuggets
Stir my soul.
I will wear the cords of honor

On the graduation day,
And promise to fulfill
My dreams of glory.
When I lead my class of peers
From these hallways of our learning,
I go confidently,
Knowing who I am.
To those of you who molded me
I give a heartfelt thanks;
I am a living testament
Unto this school of ours.

The Whole Role

My students see me in my room
So naturally they all assume
That school is the place where I must live;
They don't realize I've more to give.

Their faces light up in surprise,
Wondering looks highlight their eyes,
To see me in a grocery store
Or shopping for a new front door.

"Why teacher, teacher," they say in shock,
"You buy food? You need a lock?
You're like a real person, after all?
I never imagined you beyond the hall!"

I smile at them and say, "It's true;
There's not much difference between us two.
People are known for what they do;
School is the connection between me and you."

It's an occurrence that I take to heart;
In the play of life each has his part.
What I say and what I teach
Makes a difference to those I reach.

I'm the teacher in this situation,
The embodiment of education.
It's my ability to move beyond the role
That makes me human and leaves me whole.

Biology Lesson

I sit in the biology classroom
Trying to comprehend mitosis
But the life inside my womb
Disrupts academic thought.

Why, in spite of all I know
About cellular reproduction,
Am I pregnant with this child?
It seemed like such

An appropriate act
Between two teens in love.
My mind whispered "Consequences"
While my body screamed "Consent!"

My classmates in their innocence
See school in terms of text,
But mine is the living lesson
Of an interactive education.

Food Service

That's me with the hair net—
I cook and serve the food
With which we serve the multitudes
A balanced meal each day.

I blend a bowl of mother's love
With way too many regulations,
Mix in student tastes and wants
With the essence of good nutrition.

It's a rare thanks or compliment
I receive back for my efforts,
Yet I try each day to serve good will,
Knowing that hunger has been diminished.

Every time I see an image
Of children starving in the world,
I think of what I do each day
And spoon a smile upon each plate.

Anticipatory Set

There is an old saying about how
Those who can, do;
Those who can't—teach.
I've always taken offense at this
Notion of the inadequate.

Sometimes, though, a doubt creeps in—
Where are the rewards and stories
Of adventures wild, deals done well,
Money made in excess??

I spend my life preparing, planning:
Preparing students for the future,
Planning lessons for the week,
Preparing for a class to start,
Planning for their future's sake.

Oh, there's action in the classroom,
A constant anticipatory set;
And as the days and years roll by
I prepare the next lesson, and
Teach the art of doing.

No Point

I don't know how they expect me to learn
About geometry, history, and physical education,
When my world is collapsing around my ears
And the future is so hard to see.

My stepmom is sneaking out the back door;
Her new friend's got her sniffing white lines;
My dad's got that look like he's going ballistic—
He keeps cleaning his guns all the time.

My best friend found out she's carrying a child—
Her jerk boyfriend just dumped her last week;
Her parents are kicking her out of the house.
She's got nowhere to go but the street.

This starry eyed teacher is talking Thoreau,
Some transcendentalist philosophy bit;
Those ancient tree huggers never walked the dark side,
They should try on my shoes for a fit.

Why is it that what we cover in school
Is so far from the reality?
I see no point in studying the past
When the future is ending with me.

Labels

I didn't know that I was stupid
Until I didn't learn to read.
Then my deficiency revealed itself
Each time I saw a word.

To be different is disastrous
To a young and growing mind;
The labels and the names
Still make me cringe:

Retardeddullmoronic
Dyslexicdumbdense
Dimwittedslowilliterate:
Eachimpliesamentallack.

All I wanted was to be
Treated like a normal child.
But I realize I am different—
They can read and I can not.

In my shame I know no pride,
In my name I hear no music,
In my mind I know they're right—
I must be stupid, after all.

Music Teacher

Music is the mother tongue,
The universal wail of life,
Timeless melodies of joy and pain.

I work to teach the measured clefs,
The discipline of progressive scales,
The skills required to read the staffs.

Very few break through the forms
To find a freedom in the phrase,
Grasp the music in the notes.

Yet it is there, a sacred jewel
Within the lines of darkened dots,
Feelings coded on the page.

This is what I seek to give:
The power to unleash the song
From its bonds of ink and line

Until it rings in all its glory,
Giving voice to pain and joy,
The measure of a human soul.

Another Day

My best friend's father
Died of cancer this year.
I watched her struggle through the stages,
Grieving for her dad.
I watched the anger, the tears, the ache,
Helpless to intercede,
Insufficient to mend the tears
Ripped in the fabric of her world.

But time moves on; she's learned to hide
Personal hurt, emotional pain.
See her over there, laughing in the lounge?
You can't tell her apart from her narcissistic friends.
Oh, once in a while I see her look
At kids who know no loss,
Naive to the isolation
That marks maturity's way.

Then I go home and hug my parents,
Glad that I have yet been spared
Another day from wrenching grief and
The inevitable lamentably of death.

Cheerleader

So I have nice legs—
Does that mean I don't have a brain?
I do have to confess, sometimes
I wonder why it is I cheer.

To stand along the sidelines
Chanting inane rhymes of encouragement
Is really not too intellectual—
We're mostly background fluff and noise.

I thought it would be more glamorous–
Lipstick kisses and admiration,
Handsome high school hunks
Paying homage at my feet.

But when I put on this uniform
My exterior is on display, so
No matter what I feel inside
I smile and dance and wave.

No one asks me what I think:
I am a cheerleader, after all.

Wrong Lesson

My favorite teacher blew his brains out last week.
He left us with thoughts unformed, unsaid;
I don't really know why he did what he did,
So I've prayed for him nightly
On my knees by my bed.

But you know, God has not answered the questions I hold,
And the new teacher says that what's done is the past;
We are to look to the future, let the old slip on by,
But in my dreams I still feel the force of that blast.

The funeral is over and I guess life goes on,
But for me, it's a lesson which will last and last:
If life gets too tough, and your troubles too strong,
Get a gun, take a pill—put yourself in the past.

Copy Machine Repairman

How can a group of educators
Who control the lives of children
Be so insensitive and ignorant
Towards a finely tuned machine?

Sometimes I think that rage and temper,
Emotional frustrations from the day
Which, (in the classroom), are suppressed,
These teachers vent on the mechanical.

The step by step instructions
For clearing jams and adding toner
Seem to drive these men and women
Into illogical frames of mind.

I guess I shouldn't complain—
I earn a good living making right
What in their world is anomaly...
But I wonder—yes, I wonder--

How do they fix a broken child?

Teachers' Lounge

Welcome to the teachers' lounge,
Inner sanctum of the system,
Where teachers come to get their mail,
Eat lunch and socialize.

You wouldn't believe how important it is
To converse with an adult mind
After hours in the classroom
Where adolescence points the view.

You ought to see it at Christmas time
When everyone brings treats—
If students knew of that feast in here,
They'd understand the extra pounds.

But most of the time is it a place of refuge,
Of professional duties and information.
It's an island in a sea of kids,
A harbor from the student tides.

Sit down with me for a minute—
Pour yourself a cup of coffee—
Rest before you advance again
Into the ocean of education.

Junior High Coach

Since when did winning mean everything?
I spend my time trying to instill
A sense of fundamentals and fair play,
But it is a difficult task to teach
Teamwork to fans of TV ball.
These young players want to fly before
They've even learned to crawl,
With their three point throwups,
Reverse spin layups, and pseudo slam dunks!
They've seen Rodman play with his
Circus hair and defiant attitude,
And they want to shoot and soar just like Mike—
Never mind that they can't run a passing drill
And have never learned to break a press.
In time some of these kids will play good ball;
They will remember these nights and
Laugh at themselves while
I still sit on the bench,
Unless the irate parents get me fired first,
Or I just get tired of the games.

Student Athlete

I am a student athlete;
I claim that role with pride.
I wear the jacket of my school
With my letter on the side.

I come to class and hit the books,
Although there are things I'd rather do;
Like Odysseus of old I strive
For strength and knowledge too.

You see me on the court or field;
You cheer me when I win;
But what you should cheer most of all
Is the sports and studies blend.

I know I'll probably never be
A pro who receives high pay;
I play for love of sport—
That's why I practice every day.

I study for the future's sake—
I play sports for a different reason;
Preparing myself at every step
For a full and successful season.

The Gifted Handicap

The pace of school is excruciatingly slow—
They teach again what I already know!
And so they waste my time each day
In this school where I have to go.

I really wish there was a way
That they could hear what I have to say:
Learning for me is easy, you see;
What's work for them for me is play.

They say I'm gifted and I will be
An asset to any society;
But to me this school is just a bore—
Value in the experience I don't see.

I suppose I've learned a basic core
Of rules and info, but not much more;
When your wings are tied it's hard to soar!
So I can't wait to walk out the door,
I can't wait to stretch and roar.

History Teacher

Those who do not know history
Are doomed to repeat it—
This adage guides the tenor of my days.

I've spent my life in teaching
Others of the past we know;
Each year I repeat the lessons for the new.

A cyclical existence
In class from year to year
Has become both my blessing and my curse.

In moments of frustration
The irony assaults me:
I am victim of the very truth I teach.

It's How You Play The Game

We took the field that November eve
Blustering but scared.
Our voices had a hollow ring,
Our nerves like worn-wire bared.
All through the pregame ritual
Our doubts and fears increased,
Tearing at our confidence
Like buzzards at a feast.

We formed a ragged skirmish line
And kicked off to our foes;
Their star halfback caught the ball–
Their blockers laid us low.
On the second play of the game
They passed the ball and scored;
Their fans raised a mighty cheer—
Ours were acting bored.

Our players, small in stature,
Looked even smaller still
When pitted against their giants
Whose huddle chant was "KILL!"
That team trampled on our doubts
They rampaged o'er our fears,
And before the first half play was out
Our coach's face showed tears.

They were leading us in scoring,
Their quarterback back to toss,
When our smallest man broke through their line
And dropped him for a loss.
Yes, David nailed Goliath and
When that giant hit the ground,
He took our fears down with him
And turned the game around.

In the end the score was theirs
But we had won our fight!
We had taken fear to battle
And we learned a lot that night.
In death we are all losers
Of the game of life we play;
What counts is not the final score
But how you play along the way.

Creating the Past

I am the yearbook sponsor
And my job it is each year
To create an accurate history book
Of the memories, joys, and tears.

The potential of technology
Could make my job a breeze,
But computer glitches and deadline stress
Sometimes bring me to my knees.

My job could be so easy
If I just did the work myself;
However, I'm an educator
And I try to share the wealth

Of knowledge and techniques
That make a publication possible;
I help staff members create a book
That is fashionable, factual, and plausible.

And when each book is finally done
I swear that it's my last;
Then the school year starts again
And I'm caught up in the past.

In the Closet

I've always been different than the others
In ways at first I did not understand,
So I pretend to go along,
Echo feelings foreign to my mind.

Some of my classmates suspect, I fear,
That I am not the same as them,
That I have secrets locked inside
Which even my parents do not know.

And so I fake my way through school,
A false participant in the rites of youth,
Afraid to face the truth that flows
From the innermost part of my secret soul.

Research Paper

For four weeks I have researched,
Written, documented, and revised;
Today is the day I submit for a grade.

Now it is in the instructor's hands
And we all know he's a terror,
An error-marking fanatic from the school of quality.

He'll inspect for organization,
Documentation, development of thesis;
He'll grade it hard but fair (that's my prayer!).

Although I've griped and grumbled
About the task from time to time,
This is really what education is all about.

I've had the opportunity to
Find out what I did not know—
The subject is one of my own choosing.

No matter what the grade I get,
I've shaped my sphere of knowledge;
Now I understand more about our world.

I've completed this assignment;
For the task I should give thanks—
But right now I'm just glad the damn thing's done!

Athletic Director

When I said I'd take this job,
I really had no idea
Of the magnitude of task
That faced me that first year.
Rules and regulations,
Codes of conduct, State bylaws—
I oversee an empire
Of regulated play.

The clock is always ticking,
Time management is my old foe;
Arranging schedules years ahead
Leaves little time for now.
Emergencies demand rescheduling of
Cancelled meets and games.
Each contest has its requirements;
I navigate a paper trail.

I'm responsible for the records on every kid,
Deal with drugs and discipline,
Arrange to move my teams each way,
Organize schedules so all runs smooth.
Amidst the grind and hustle bustle
A tiny thought rears its head;
In my busy life of helping others—
In my busy life of getting things done—

Did I spend enough time
With my own kids today?

Guitar Star

I know that I am in school to learn
But few of the subjects make my soul burn.
Most of the classes seem like a waste;
They don't satisfy my educational taste.

But put a guitar in my hands,
Teach me the history of rock and roll bands,
Offer me a course on effects and amps,
Drill me in rock riffs, scales, and vamps;

Then you'll see me come alive.
It's from this passion I derive
The essence of my bliss inside,
The goose bump thrills of a musical ride.

Hendrix, Clapton, B.B. King—
These are names to me that ring
The inner workings of my heart;
Their music sings to my life and art.

So understand—I'm different than you
In the things I want to learn and do.
Don't put me down—I have my star,
And to there I'll fly with my guitar.

School Secretary

I may be just a secretary,
But in reality I run the school.
Oh, I'm not the one who makes the rules,
Nor do I sign my name to checks.
My office squats outside the suite
Where the chief administrators sit.

But when you want to get something done
It's me who does the work.
I smooth the way to the big desk,
Shuffle papers to grant requests.
Students and teachers both growl,
Frustrated if I'm not here—
Telephones keep on ringing,
Schedules quickly fall apart.

Like others, I am worth
Much more than what I'm paid.
But my pride in a job done well
Keeps me at my post.
I am essential to the system,
And my smile can make your day.

The Janitor's Last Day on the Job

I've worked at this school for half my life;
Now it is my time to simplify.
In these halls I've heard laughs,
Seen hot scalding tears,
Discovered secrets best left unsaid.

A friend gave me advice on my very first day:
"Kids can make life a heaven or hell—
Treat them with respect; it will return many fold."
I've tried to abide by that nugget of truth.

As I leave here I offer these words:
Do unto others better than they would you;
Be not afraid to humble yourself;
No job is worth more than the person who does it.

Official

I wear the striped shirt at night
Judge black and white from shades of grey,
Race up and down the wood floor court
Shrilly whistling wrong from right.

I was an athlete myself,
Lived for the glory of the game;
When I could no longer participate
I certified to adjudicate.

The fans rarely appreciate
The decisive calls I have to make;
When I whistle against the home team stars,
The crowd will sometimes retaliate.

As in so many games of life
My role is without much glamour;
But without the ruling arm of law,
Chaos would quickly conquer.

Final Exam

I am the measure and milestone of learning,
The test of achievement in education.
Watch the students study and stress—
They know the power of my probing questions.

Concentration furrows the forehead brow.
Fingers clutch the marking pens,
Fly across the keyboard commands,
Distilling the essence of what is known.

Words and ideas—all abstraction,
Reduced to quick choices of expression.
Careers are built upon my artifice—
The final accomplishment recorded as grade.

Phys Ed Teacher

I teach play—that's what some say,
Although I doubt they really understand
How the long term pay will arrive some day
When happiness and health go hand in hand.

Benefits accrue with the exercise you do;
To be active is a goal that each should set.
My class provides the clue for the physically fit crew:
Healthy mind and bodies are the best bet yet.

Please Ask

Please don't ask how my day went.
I know I'm fat and stupid and ugly—
My father tells me so.
He says I'll never be as smart as him
And he never finished school.

Please don't ask about my family.
My mother's been in prison for three long years.
My father divorced her.
I get to see her once a month, six hours at a time,
If my father will take me there-
Which he doesn't like to do.
My brother doesn't talk much—
He just got out of jail—
And my only sister ran away.
That just leaves me at home—with Dad.

Please don't ask about my father.
He works most nights, so I'm alone
Until the early morning hours
When he sometimes wakes me
With his wet wishes and desires.
I tell myself that if I go along
He'll really need and love me—
At least he's not mean for a little while.

Please don't ask me why I fail.
I try, but just can't concentrate.
I guess I'm stupid like he says,
And I know I'm fat and ugly too;
I just wish someone cared.

Prejudice

I am the insidious monger of hate,
Manifesting myself in racial pride.
Dissension is my aim in life;
Intolerance is my ugly bride.

Fostering fear and internal strife,
Colorblind, we make our rounds.
I love an argument over who is best;
My scorn for humanity knows no bounds.

I'll sow the seeds before I rest
That will grow into a violent fate,
And then I will laugh at the stupid fools
Who have swallowed hook, line, sinker, and bait.

Government Teacher

My job it is to teach the workings
Of the government of the United States;
To examine the different powers in
Executive, judicial, legislative;
It is a daunting duty in the realm of day to day.

The actions of the players in the political arena
Are often muddied by the effluence
Which soils their hands and deeds,
Yet I am educating minds noted for their idealism
Which are quick to note the disparity
Between what is said and what is seen.

So I do the best I can to show
What the Constitution means,
Then temper it with discussions
Of what transpires on Capitol Hill,
At least as far as what the media shows.

It is the essence of civic democracy,
This information I disseminate;
Our future as a nation rests upon these principles.
Yet the disillusioned apathy of the present generation
Makes me wonder just how long
This government will last.

Counselor

My office is a whirlwind
Of scholarships and tears,
The dirty laundry piles behind my door.

Child abuse and alcohol,
Sex and tawdry tales
Squat amidst the backdrop of school dreams.

Sometimes I just wish
That they didn't feel so free
To tell me of their problems and their fears.

Yet every opportunity
To help should be explored,
Every avenue of trust opened wide.

For every dream up in the air
I see one fall away,
Shattered by the vagaries of life.

Choices become critical to
Health and wealth and learning—
Every door that opens has its price.

I can make suggestions and
Guide by push and shove,
But there are limits to what I can and cannot do.

In the end they must decide
What they should do themselves;
The sanctity of choice must be preserved–

And that is what's so difficult to know.

The System

School systems have their faults—
Almost every system does—
They work about as well as the people
In them do.
I work within the system
So I can do the most good
For the children and the students
That I serve.

To show a human being
The joy of learning more than content
Is why I work at teaching
In this school.
I work with individuals
Within a larger group setting,
Trying to instill the love of learning
In their hearts.

Oh, I really don't agree
With all of the rules and regulations,
Which I know do help preserve
The common good.
But as a member of the system
I have access to a world
That extends beyond the limits
Of my reach.

My job won't make me wealthy
In the material sense of the world,
But I trust that what I do will
Make a difference.

Old Guard

I've been in this school for 29 years,
Seen principals and superintendents come and go,
Seen the kids I've taught grow up and move on—
Now I'm teaching the kids of those kids.

Seen a lot of changes in the years of my time.
Remember when we had the blue ditto machine?
Now it's all computers and copiers and internet mail,
Hardly time for a hot cup of coffee in the lounge.

The pay's gotten better, but I still don't have much:
A car needing tires, and a house with fading paint.
The money I've saved is put aside in a fund—
Someday I'll use it, but I've done without for so long.

Yes, I guess that life has really been good;
I'm not rich, but I still like the job that I do.
I notice that I'm more tired at the end of the day,
Guess it's about time for the changing of the guard.

But I hate the thought of just fading away,
And I don't know that I want to be anything else.
So maybe I will hang on for another year or two;
What would I do if I didn't go to school?

Serving Time in ISS

Now I'm really not a bad kid at all,
Sometimes I just make mistakes,
Like when me and two friends took off from school,
After we pulled our illness fakes.
We ended up out at the mall,
Checking out the electronic games
And I can't really say it was a surprise
When the school PA blared out our names.

Yea, you know that we got caught
And the principal read us the rules,
Assigned us a makeup day of time—
Suspended, but still in school.
Now we didn't fight and we didn't steal,
We didn't drink beer and we sure didn't deal;
The only thing we did that was wrong—
We were somewhere else than where we belonged.

Serving time for an in-school suspension
Isn't really all that tough;
Except after a while the clock slows down
And the boredom becomes rather rough.
Our classmates are going about their lives,
Able to wander from class to hall,
While here we sit, locked in a room,
Waiting for the seconds to fall.

You know, time is relative to most folks,
That's what old Einstein said;
And until I spent some time locked up
The meaning never entered my head.
But God! how slow these minutes go;
Time right now is dragging!
The clock has melted into the wall,
The face and hands are sagging.

Those few hours that we skipped
Were definitely less long
Than the amount of time we're making up—
Something about this formula is wrong!
But we are guilty, I admit,
And I guess we'll do our time.
I've learned one lesson out of this—
A wasted day is the real crime.

Librarian

It used to be the printed word
That filled my room and shelves;
Books and books and books were mine
To place within the decimal system.

But the card catalogue files are gone,
Replaced by electronic technology,
And the magazines which lined the racks
Are dwindling every year.

My realm has become an access site
Where students log on and out,
Interacting in a cyber world
Where information is traded freely.

I miss the comfort of a book well used,
The classic feel of knowledge bound;
Elements of a world I love,
Old technology from the printing press.

The evolution of our changing times
Threatens to overwhelm my role,
And leave it behind on shelf and stacks,
Like neglected volumes from the past.

Substitute Teacher

Sometimes in the early morn
When I'm awakened by the ringing phone,
The voice which pleads, "Will you teach today?"
Then I wonder who has called in sick,
And decide to hedge a cautious reply.

I see the worst, sometimes the best
Of teaching in the area schools.
After an hour in another's shoes,
I can tell you much about their teaching style.

To walk into a foreign room,
To command respect and discipline
While working through the hasty plans—
These are skills for which most have
Neither the ability nor the temperament.

I've had the chance to teach full time
And someday I may accept again;
But for now I will simply place my name
And exercise the right to pick and choose.

A Teaching Model

All of us are teachers,
Yet not all of us can teach;
It takes much more to help someone
Than a propensity to preach.
Exciting others is the key
To making learning real;
It's how you inspire those you teach
That is really the big deal.

Pain and pleasure are two tools
Which history has shown
Are motivating factors in what is
Learned and what is known.
Let's face it: fear's effective,
But it's not the preferred way
Of encouraging minds to seek
Knowledgeable solutions for the day.

Kindness is an asset, and
Although its presence should be a rule,
Discipline is also necessary,
Both in life and here at school.
Threats and violence are subordinated
To altruistic desire;
But it almost always takes a match
To light the learning fire.

We lead by prime examples;
Texts and resources provide many clues
To help in educating others
In what our world would have them do.
At the base lies human nature;
This fact must not be lost
If we're to polish up the process,
Take the steps, afford the cost

Of producing human beings
Who can feel, think, choose, and talk;
Freedom is the bottom line—
All the rest are building blocks.
Actions speak much louder than words—
What you do tells who you are.
That's what life is all about—
Understand this, and you'll go far.

The Fight

It really didn't start out as much—
She called my little sister names;
I warned her not to keep it up,
She pushed me back into my words.

I grabbed a lock of wiry hair,
She clawed me with her fingernails—
Then our fists began to fly;
Blood splattered on the carpeted floor.

If I'd had a knife, I would have pulled it;
If she'd had a gun, she would have used it.
I wanted that witch dead—
She, too, was scared enough to kill.

I wish I could apologize,
Restore the blood which soured our lives;
Redeem the deeds of aggression,
Protect the weak from becoming prey.

Instead I must remain on guard,
Watch my back, lock my door;
Worry about the uneasy truce,
Learn the cost of waging war.

Not Enough Time

I try to hide my naked head,
Duck imprecations, besieging questions;
I know each query is a caring concern,
But I'm tired of odd looks and pity.

The cancer creeps in, a relentless stormsurge—
X-rays, scans, biopsies, chemotherapy—
I endeavor to keep the children on task,
Submerge my grief in a flurry of lessons.

It is comforting to think my memory lives,
Etched in the minds of these young;
I only wish I could reach each one and
Turn back the inexorable shadows of time.

Foreign Language Instructor

Those who think in only one
Of the world's most basic tongues
Don't know the limitations they
Bring to their own minds each day.

Sounds reflect the way a brain
In words and rhetoric can be trained.
So widen out your point of view—
Learn a language new to you!

There's more to life than what you know;
Please—try not to let your naiveness show.
You should visit other lands,
Learn their cultures if you can.

But most of all, understand
That in this creature we call man,
Language is the connecting link
Of what we see, share, feel, and think.

Publications Room

Deadlines are my lifeblood,
A time when I vibrate with vitality;
The crunch is on again.
The staff works frantically,
Intent on reaching assignment goals.

This is when snap decisions are made—
What to run, what to kill.
Editors review the pages,
Piece together layouts and design,
Pick up the slack when someone falls.

The rush to publish invigorates.
Desktop stations are all occupied;
Proofreaders pore over the pages.
Headlines scramble for attention
As photographs are scanned and placed.

Then it is over, distributed at last.
Staff writers linger over used copy,
Dawdling as their efforts become old news.
Even as they breathe a small sigh of respite,
Deadlines form to immerse them once again.

Homecoming Queen

I know what you're thinking–
No, it's not like that at all.
I'm not a snot and I'm not stuck up–
I'm not some barbie doll.

I have brains and personality–
I just happen to have that look
Which to the world says that I'm sexy,
Although I'd rather curl up with a book.

I didn't campaign for this honor–
The student body voted, you know;
I resent your insinuation
That I'm some empty headed bimbo.

Sometimes nice girls finish first–
If you don't like it, leave me be.
I won't be something that I'm not
Just to fulfill your fantasy.

Runner Up

I can't believe she won the crown!
What'd she do, sleep with them all?
I am much prettier, with my silky blond hair,
And I tried so hard to be nice this month.

Here I sit, a neglected princess,
While she gets the hugs and smiles.
Hey you, take my picture—
I'm the one who deserves the title!

I can't believe the stupidity
Of students who voted for her—
She hasn't half of what I have,
If people really knew.

So here I sit and make small talk
With the others who lost as well;
We smile our smiles behind jealous eyes
And wish we were wearing the crown.

Alumni

I didn't remember until I walked back in
How a school has a special smell.
The wave of memory washes over me;
My mind replays the experience of education:

Laughs and lectures, lockers and lunch,
The lonely sound of footsteps in the halls.
Trophy cases ring with the hollow cheers of distance.
Benign colors bind perennial classrooms.

Only the faces have changed.
Where are the salutes, the styles which were so familiar?
Have they all gone? Have I gone too?
What is this emptiness here in my heart?

My past is buried in this present.
Does anyone even remember my name?

Drama Director

All the world's a stage, he says,
And we all are but players;
My role, however, requires me
To stage plays with earthbound talent.

To see them jerk and stammer
Before the curtain the first time
Would make one less assured
Doubt the wisdom of my task.

But we learn the lines assiduously—
I give hints to help interpret—
And what was merely wooden speech
Finally flows from protege's tongue.

And thus I start a first run show
Between youth and a stage new trod;
I direct the drama of student life—
The production is playing still.

Football Coach

I am the coach of the football team;
Those are my boys out there.
You might say I'm the commanding general–
I direct my boys with flair.

Up and down the field we play,
Offense charging for a goal,
Until the tide of score or war
Shoves us back into the hole.
Then the defense takes the field
To stop the run and pass;
We strive to control the scrimmage line
With smarts, speed, muscle, and mass.

It's a game of strength, guile, and skill;
Quick thinking is an asset;
And I work hard to prepare my team—
We practice every facet.

On any given night or day
A team could lose or win;
But conditioning and preparedness
Are two places to begin.
And as for that, I instill pride
And a fierce desire to compete;
Qualities that change boys to men,
Help make their lives complete.

Some say this sport is savagery,
Brutal jocks in lines of battle;
But I know better—these young men play
A sport that proves their mettle.

Dropout

I don't need this crap
To make it on my own!
What use is English class
To a hustlin' guy like me?
What will a government course
Teach me about a job?
I'd like to see the principal
Bundle shingles up a roof!
Which of them can frame a house,
Fix a truck, wire a light?
No, their school is for the brain bound,
And I've not time for that.
I'm getting out while I still can
Before they wreck my life.

Science Teacher

Getting them to see the connections—
That's the hardest part.
They read the text, learn the terms,
Memorize formulas and principles
Necessary for test scores and recitations;
But teaching applications—
That's the secret to what I do.

The world in which we work and play
Operates on applications,
Every product engineered
According to what we know and observe.
It's one thing to use a tool,
Something else to understand it—
I try to bridge the gap between utilize and know.

To teach why which and what works how
Is my philosophy of education;
I embrace the mystery of life
With scientific explanation.
All is knowable if we supercede
The limitations of our expectations.
My point of reference is the working world;
I elucidate the complications.

A Lesson in Ethics

It wasn't any big deal—I hadn't finished math,
So I borrowed a friend's paper and
Took the easy path.
It wasn't but two problems; I was almost through
When a shadow fell upon me and suddenly I knew
That I had been caught cheating,
An action that was wrong.
I looked up at the teacher's face;
I knew he wouldn't go along.
Suddenly the day went dark,
In my ears hissed a sad song.

At home my father talked of trust, integrity and lies;
I thought he was making way too much of what,
In my simplistic eyes, was just a
Common occurrence— kids cheat every day.
But when we finished talking,
I saw things in a different way.
So now I have a standard to which
I'll forge strong bonds anew;
My work will always be my own—
I won't do as others do.
I'll accept the consequences of my actions
Each and every day,
And do my best in school and life
No matter what others say.

I will not cheat—I will not lie.
My integrity will be my shield.
Although I know it's a constant war,
My honesty I will not yield.
So I guess this little incident really
Served some good that day;
It made me find integrity—
From that path I will not stray.
Actions tell us more through deeds
Than words can ever say—
I was caught cheating once—
Never again will I take that way.

Friends and classmates—please be true.
When you cheat a part of you dies—
Strive for honor and dignity too
And don't ever live by lies.

Unnatural Selection

The news has made much of teen violence,
Shows the killing of kids by kids;
You know, bring an automatic weapon,
Pack a pistol, or a knife well hid.

How about the tobacco companies,
Featuring Joe Camel and all of the gang?
They want you to light up and take a puff—
It's a hit of cancer with a deadly bang!

And then there are the car wrecks,
Slippery curves of wine, whiskey, and beer—
Have another one for the road.
Have a shot and conquer your fear!

Suicide is a big killer—if done well,
Nobody escapes alive.
AIDS is the secret eliminator
That sneaks in on over-sexed drive.

I say its all natural selection—
Most of us live, but some die.
Not everyone gets a second chance;
Tough luck, so long, bye-bye!

Snow Day

The forecast is for storms and snow,
A blizzard, perhaps, with winds that blow
Icy crystals into drifts which grow—
What this means all students know.

The possibility of an extra day
Where demands of school are far away,
When nature holds us in her sway—
This is for what the pupils pray.

The roads are slick with snow and ice;
To travel now is not good advice.
The ones in charge have to think twice:
Is school attendance worth the price?

And so we get a break from school;
This winter storm is way too cruel
To venture out and play the fool—
Young life is such a precious jewel.

Nature's storms are among the best
To determine survival, the ultimate test;
The surprise of a snowday is a guest
That stands apart from the scheduled rest.

The Dilbert Principal: a disgruntled employee disses his boss.

It's ironic, you know,
How those who teach poorly
Are often the ones who
Advance up the ladder.

Slipping into an administrative position,
They have the power
To squelch what is good.

From behind the desk,
They rule their small world
Dispensing decrees of minor importance.

They hide behind fear and
A bully mentality,
Nasty large fish in a tiny cool pool.

There they will reign,
Avoiding real problems,
Dodging and ducking
Until retirement comes.

Committees

Meetings, meetings—
Always more meetings.
We sit down hurriedly,
Flip open lifetime planners,
Examine stacked agendas.
It is time to begin to
Compartmentalize our thoughts.

Lives are set aside, personal
Problems ignored as we focus
The task on the table before us.
Rarely is there time to talk
About matters of primordial importance—
Instead we attend the minutiae,
Detailing cogs of the internal machine.

At the end of one session we're off to another,
A reoccurring series of rippled affairs.
Individuals drop off in the shuffle of time.
Members atrophy along the way,
Replaced by new blood, drafted to serve.
Only the task and committee endure,
Stuck in a meeting of similar minds.

School Bus Driver

See that yellow bus outside?
Well, that's my vehicle,
Yea, that's my ride.
Hauling kids is what I do
To school and games and
On field trips too.
It's pretty fun, but sometimes loud;
It all depends
Upon the crowd.
Now I'm not the fastest rig around;
I have to halt often
And let kids down.
So when you see that red sign swing,
And the flashing lights
Warn "Bus Stopping,"
Just sit back, think what you've learned;
Let the students get off,
You wait your turn.
Your role is to keep your cool,
Let those kids get
To and from school.

Obey the rules and back off, Jack!
Cut me and my yellow bus
Some slack.
Safety is what's on my mind,
Take your foot off the gas and
Stay behind.
You could never replace the life of a child;
Use some common sense–
Don't drive wild.
Play it safe and don't cause a fuss;
Have some respect
For that yellow school bus.

New Tattoo

Check it out, man, my new tattoo,
Just had it needled in yesterday.
Made an appointment at the Parlour,
Black Celtic cross on grey.

Don't really know what it means,
But hey, ain't it cool!
I'm a patron of the arts,
The most decorated dude in school!

Life ain't just about using your head—
A guy's got to look sharp, too!
I might not make the honor roll,
But I'm recognized for what I do.

Yea, I made a statement about myself,
It's right there on my arm.
Trust the system if you want,
But for me, it's looks and charm!

Shop Teacher

I've seen a lot of changes
In the classes that I teach;
Few want to learn the old ways
Of working with their hands.

Computers now are all the rage;
Technology is the buzz word.
Heck, I've been teaching that for years;
What do they think a tool is?

My department has changed, though,
To keep up with the times
That the experts in education
Say is just around the corner.

Still, the silky feel of sanded wood
No cyberclass can show,
And the lessons learned by hands-on work
No keyboard stroke can copy

A man's body is a work of God,
A finely made tool a miracle of mind.
When we neglect our abilities to build,
We toss away the keys to heaven.

Jock

Sometimes I think I'd like school more
If ancient Sparta had won the war.
Then my goal in life would be
To overcome my enemy.

I could train my muscled arm
To wreak havoc and cause foes harm.
I could strive both night and day
In games of strength and deadly play.

But no, they insist I use my brains
For abstract math and word refrains.
The world has advanced to a state
Where personal strength does not relate.

And yet I long for days of yore
When a man knew what his strength was for.
Maybe again there will come a time
When body triumphs over mind.

Until that day I'll struggle on,
But to a different world belong.

Support Group

Each Thursday afternoon we meet
To talk and help each other,
The six of us who are the core
Of the girls at-risk support group.
Others come and go at whim
But we've sworn to stick together.
What is said is not repeated—
We are the only ones we trust.

We talk of many different things,
Of rumors, sex, and problems:
Abusive guys, friends who use,
The lure of suicide.
Each secret shared is a sacred bond
Served to sever isolation;
By airing out our hidden fears,
We learn that others alleviate
The horrors that assault us.

The hour passes all too quickly
To heal the hurts and wounds,
So when we leave we close our selves,
Our pain tucked deep inside us.
Our problems haven't gone away,
But through sharing, our burden shifted.

Wrong Questions

I flunked another test again.
The questions covered some assigned readings;
I was told to write everything I know
About subjects I could care less for.

Why don't they ask me about something
That I really want to know,
Instead of algebra and literature,
Or the way cells multiply?

Ask me about cool computer games,
Or how to survive the asphalt jungle.
Ask me about working nights
To make payments on my car.

Ask me about my parents' divorce
Or the parties on the weekend.
Just make the subject interesting—
Or I'll probably flunk again.

Special Ed Teacher

My love for every form of life
Led me to this calling;
The sacredness of the human spirit
Is what I strive for every day.

The little things are what I live for:
The look of recognition, a shy smile of success,
Indications that the light of learning
Has pushed away the darkness.

Others don't see the beauty
In the souls I try to aid.
Stuck on the superficial,
They hurry past my room.

If they could only see themselves,
They'd stop to wonder why
Their compassion ends so abruptly,
Why they don't acknowledge the pain.

If only they'd stop and look around,
Give recognition to the lives who
Want so desperately for acceptance,
Who wish a new world to unfold.

The beauty of a simple task
The joy of comprehension
The wonder of achievement
The awe-ful miracle of life.

All Prejudice Aside

I know I may not look like you,
But my blood runs red when spilled.
So in spite of superficialities,
We are brothers, sisters all.

Forget the differences in hair and lips,
Shades of skin or angle of eye;
What matters is the way we treat the other,
Our neighbors like our selves.

If you want a fight I'll give you one,
But I'd rather we get along;
Just don't shove your prejudice
Into the world we both must share.

Can you imagine the inane boredom
In a world of only gray?
So let's celebrate the differences,
Search for rainbows in the sky.

Value me because I'm not like you—
Yet when you look into my eyes,
See the reflection of yourself,
And know we really are the same.

Drivers Education

"Come on—let's go for a ride!"
Do you realize the implications?
You're crawling into a rocket ship—
Just how capable is your guide?

Do you know what speed and metal mass
Can do to human tissue?
When you slide behind the driver's wheel
Do you know when and where to pass?

Do you observe the rules of the road?
Do you obey the highway signs?
You are going to make quick judgment calls;
Can you guarantee the safety of your load?

Wheels provide flight, a free bird risen,
That we drivers often take for granted.
But if you make a mistake and end up in a wreck,
You might find the grave is your final prison.

Retirement

For over thirty years I've taught the essence of what I know
To a river of fresh-faced children who receive, then move away.
This morning the face in the bathroom mirror spoke to me of change.
The greying hair and wrinkled skin reminded me of progressing age,
And even though I love my job, I wonder if it's not time
To let someone else take my classes, step down from my career.

I've always sworn that I would know when it was time to quit,
That when I heard myself complain about the role in life I play,
It would be time to reassess my goals, to evaluate just where I stand.

The children of children past populate my room.
I see their faces superimposed upon the roster of the years.
Sometimes I stop to remind myself not to mix the sibling names,
Even though I see their elders in the faces of the young.

What would I do if I don't teach? Who would fill my shoes?
Yet I know that each must pass outward through the doors,
That to graduate each stage in life is part of what I know.
I have acquaintances who would not hesitate to
Depart these hallowed walls,
Who would jump to leave career behind,
Embrace golf and leisure time.

The thought of waking up with nothing specific to do each day
Scares me just a little, although it has attractions, too.
Would I be just another senior waiting out the years?

So I must make a decision—
Carry on in spite of age like an old horse in the harness,
Or plunge into a twilight world to create myself again?
What have I learned that will help me decide?

School Rules

Of all the possibilities in life,
I chose to be a teacher—
I could have been a scientist,
I could have been a preacher—
But I decided to work with kids,
To show them what they need
To blossom intellectually,
Grow a flower from a seed.

To me there is no greater joy
Than bringing enlightenment
Where once only darkness reigned
Without educational commitment.
To turn a light on in a mind
Is the desire of my heart,
To make someone see the whole
When they had only known a part.

And at end of day when I lay down,
I hope and pray that I have brought
Through books and opportunities
A measure of learning to those I've taught.
It's a sacred calling to those of us
Who've made our world that place called school,
A responsibility that comes with every day
When we've lived and taught the golden rule.

Fellowship of Christian Athletes

I am a Christian and an athlete;
I let the Bible be my guide
As I live my days in glory
On the courts and fields of pride.

I seek to find an appropriate mix
Of "Turn the cheek" and "Win!";
The principles of my religious beliefs
Are at odds with the aggression of sin.

But through my actions, deeds, and words,
I let Christ's light shine through;
He sacrificed his life for us,
Died on cross to redeem me and you.

So judge me if you must–
I stand square behind my Lord.
My beliefs will be my armor
As I face the worldly horde.

Gym Floor

It took acres of trees to make this gym floor—
You can feel their vibrancy in a bouncing ball,
Test the tension with sole of sneaker.

The lines run straight in perfect seams,
Parallel in widths beyond nature's design,
Ordered and ranked like an unnatural forest.

Games of skill are played on this surface,
Level plane of existential existence,
Layer upon layer over nature's bedrock.

This floor is a dimensional wooden base
Upon which energy swirls and flows,
Man's order imposed upon life's natural growth.

Math Teacher

My office is the busiest during seminar,
When students come to me for help.
Somehow these mathematical concepts
Are hard for many to grasp.

I work problems on the board,
Answer questions and demonstrate,
Explain again and yet again
The formulas and procedures.

Higher mathematics is an abstract science
Which builds upon itself.
Without a mastery of algebraic formula
The principles just don't add up.

Sine and cosine, tangential equations,
Imaginary numbers and probability,
Calculus, trigonometry, negative values—
All are clear to the well trained mind.

From counting on fingers to applying quantum mechanics,
The story of mathematics chronicles
The rise of the modern technological world,
Our society of numbers.

What is so difficult about that?

Football Stadium

It's silent now, but they will return,
The fans who cheer the players on.
The seats will come alive again,
Roar into the ebb and flow
As players dash across the field.

It's silent now, but wars are staged on this green gridiron.
Coaches stride along the side,
Barking orders to the troops,
Striving for that elusive elixir
Which will win them points or turf.

It's silent now, as the wind blows cold,
But again the giant lights will blaze.
Night is vanquished by the light.
Fears are forced into shadows dark,
Where they lurk and sulk and plot a return.

It's silent now—the ghosts of teams and players past
Weakly chant the cold grey dawn in voices
Muted by envelopes of memory.
They will return—and again the lights of
Friday night will offer respite from silence.

Early Enlistment

When my senior year is done and graduation over,
I will leave the academic world and join the military.
Then is when my education will truly begin anew.

Until that time I will study my assignments,
Laugh with my classmates, cut up in the halls,
Act as though I am no different than any one of
them.

In my mind, though, I march to a beating drum
Which few of my friends will ever hear within their
lives;
It is a call to service, to wear the uniform with pride.

Mine is the warrior's journey, an occupation old
Which foster's strength of mind and might of arm;
A decisive path through a noble past to a future
bright with honor.

Attendance Officer

Every hour I check the school
To see who's here and who isn't;
My job it is to keep the stats
On the tardies and the absent.

Some students profess to view the school
As a prison to escape from;
They're the ones who don't agree
That education is a mutual concern.

So I record the skips each day,
Along with doctor's excuses and tardies,
Assign detention and make-up time
In an effort to teach attendance.

To run free without an itinerary
Is a dream that we all flirt with,
But it's a path that leads to emptiness—
Why can't these students see this?

Society demands accountability
From citizens and leaders both;
We try to reinforce the lesson here:
Students don't succeed when they're gone.

Teacher's Kid

My father is a teacher at the school where I attend,
So that makes me a teacher's kid,
A role of mixed reviews.
It really helps with homework—I've access to a tutor,
But it's hard to escape notice when
I'd really rather hide.
He sees my friends, hears what I do,
Checks up on me in class—
Like Santa Claus he always knows
When I've been good or bad.
Sometimes he embarrasses me;
I don't want to be related,
Like when he tells an awful joke,
Or forgets to zip his fly.
Sometimes his breath smells really bad,
Like coffee three days old.
And when he piles the homework on,
The students gripe at me.
But I see his love of teaching in the way
He treats the kids,
And deep inside I'm really proud
Of how he does his job.
And in the end the perks
Outweigh the disadvantages of my condition;
So call me a teacher's kid if you want—
You're just jealous of my position!

Principal

They see me in my office,
Authority behind the desk,
As I assign the disciplines
To the breakers of the rules.

Most don't know the leadership
Manifested on the system:
The complexity of schedules
Which affect school, staff, and students.
I balance needs of people
With the directives of the board,
Make decisions on the budget line,
Manage mandates, curriculum, and goals.

I am a walking target
For every patron with a gripe;
Some nights I do not sleep at all
Thinking thoughts best left unsaid.

But in the morning hours when
I rise before the sun,
I feel the call and know my life
Has been the right choice after all:
A student's smile, a thank you note
From a kid who straightened out,
A graduate who shakes my hand,
The respect of staff and friends.

These are survival strategies
In a life of conflict and reports:
Pick the battles wisely,
And know I form the future.

Grounds for Dismissal

It's quite amazing what some students do
Just to gain an academic grace.
Why, I've seen the curve of budding breasts
Thrust suggestively in my face;
A nubile nymph suggesting love,
A handsome youth offering lust's embrace.

The nether regions below the mind
Can offer temptations hard to resist.
Academic improvement is sometimes sought
By one who lays hands on your wrists,
Who tugs and pulls in sensuous ways,
Begging to be fondled and kissed.

Anyone going to such extremes
(It's enough to turn a virtuous head!)
Should undoubtedly receive an interim grade
And through deceptive halls be led
In private to an inner sanctum
Where moral behavior is put to bed.

It's as old as life, this game they play
Where credit is offered and received;
I've seen it working dozens of times,
In ways that are hard to believe.
Yes, it's the story of sex for sale—
Yet let not the participants be deceived.
There are layers of moral behavior
Which the unwary might suddenly find.
What is traded for a few moments pleasure
Is often not easily left behind.
Experience is not always education;
Lust will not always subvert the mind.

Student Teacher

I started this program on fire,
Sure that I could make a difference;
Anxious to prove myself no
Ordinary brick in the wall.

I mastered psychology and methods,
Learned ed history inside out,
Promulgated philosophies of education,
Observed and thought and wrote.

Now I'm in the classroom bowl
And nothing is as clear
As it looked from on the outside
Before the class was mine.

When this trial is over
(I just pray that I survive!)
I will know better what to keep
And which part to throw away.

All the theory in the world
Can't replace experience—
I may claim the teacher title,
But my learning's just begun.

Quiet Ones

I am one of the quiet ones
Who move through school unrecognized,
No verbal handpats from the staff,
No awards or honors on the boards.

In class I choose a seat in back,
Never speak or raise my hand,
Work just enough to get the grade,
Don't look the teacher in the eye.

Yet I envy those who are singled out,
Although I would probably die from shame,
Collapse red faced under scrutiny—
Still it is my secret wish.

But that will never happen—
Not for me the teacher's smile!
Just a bland face in the crowd,
My name on the roster—that's all.

Funeral

The organist is playing softly—slow, sad songs.
We file past the casket, find a seat near the back row,
Watch the church fill up with friends and family of
      the dead.
Each one is a chapter or a footnote to the life
Which lies cold lipped and silent,
A book closed upon itself.
If only we could have gathered while the spark of life
      still flickered,
So that before death settled he could see the
Many facets of flame and fire
Gathered at the grave in personal tribulation.
The minister speaks of celebrating the short life
      which has ended,
But the eulogy pales against the memory
Like a candle fades in light.
Life was here, now it is gone—
We pause to note the passage,
Then leave with uncertainty by our side.
It is not natural for the old to bury the young.
The irony of the elders mourning this passage
Swirls on the air like flakes of ash,
Pages of a burning book.

School Nurse

Cuts and coughs and runny noses
Are my domain in school;
Every child with a surface wound
Comes to see me and be healed.

I patch the scrapes and check the temps,
Soothe fevered brows and tear-stained cheeks;
If all my patients were so simply treated,
My job would be a breeze.

It's the wounds which lie deeper
That keep me awake at night:
The high school girl with a STD,
The boy with needle tracks,

At-risk behaviors which allow disease
To invade the susceptible young,
Ruin immune systems, wreak havoc on health;
These cases haunt my dreams.

Underneath the calm I wear like a halo,
My heart cries out for these tortured souls;
The band aids I have to offer
Won't heal their world of hurt.

The New Home Economics

You won't find a lot of abstract theory
In my lesson plans;
The courses are designed to teach life skills,
In answer to real demands.
Concepts of nutrition,
Reproduction, social norms,
Are served with practicality
And a knowledge of life's forms.

The greatest difficulty in my classes
That I have to overcome
Are the stereotypes of Heloise—
You know, classes for the mentally numb.
The skills I teach are essential
To living a quality life;
We strive to combat ignorance
With which the world is rife.

So welcome to my classroom
But enter with an open mind.
I teach life applications—
Please leave old stereotypes behind.

Superintendent

Few know the price of leadership;
It's a rarefied air at the top.
Most just see the salary
And think I have it made.

I walk the line in two worlds:
Director of staff, leader of the BOE;
Answerable to the bottom line,
Balancing innovation and performance.

I defuse the volatile, dull the axes,
Assess the validity of complaints,
Protect the needs of my personnel
From detractors who don't have a clue.

My personal life is swallowed up
By the professional role I play;
Like a handshaking politician I don't stop
Until the district is left far behind.

The responsibility of education
Is always foremost on my mind;
I fuel the torch of the future
From the sparks of day to day.

An Art

I want to paint, she says.
I want to sculpt, he says.
I applaud the ambition which has brought you here,
But first you must learn to draw a line.

This is too boring, he says.
This is too slow, she says.
I know you think you are ready to run,
But first you must learn to crawl, then walk.

Art is too hard, he says.
Art is too demanding, she says.
I know the frustration of wanting to create,
But of not having the skills to express your talent.

Come see what I've done, she says.
This is just what I wanted, he says.
I see the techniques you have mastered at last,
I admire your creation. This is an art.

School Board

We meet at times convenient—
Night meetings are the rule—
To take care of the business
Of the running of the school.
Some of us wear business suits,
Others of us work in jeans;
All of us have concerns at heart
About education and what it means.

So we follow rules of order,
Discuss the issues near at hand,
Make long range goals for the future,
Affect the present in ways we can.
We deal with budgets, staff, and policy,
Talk of sums beyond our means,
Approve programs in the lower grades,
Affect the lives of countless teens.

It's a task that taxes imagination
Requiring stamina, vision, and skills;
The irony of the situation is
It's a position a vote still fills.

Janitor

Some kid stuffed paper towels
In the toilet bowl again.
The restroom floor is flooded;
To the rescue I must come.
This, on top of all the other duties
I must get done in a day,
Makes me wonder why I serve
This unappreciative juvenile crowd.

It's more than just the money—
There's so much that I could do
To feed my family, pay the bills,
That would not get my hands dirty.
But I spend my days and nights
Picking up the district trash,
Wiping out the traces
Of a careless culture's passing:

Cleaning out the bleachers
After games on weekday nights,
Changing lightbulbs, sweeping halls,
Wiping chalkboards after class.
Sisyphus in his labors had
No more to do than I,
Current tasks barely finished
When my workday begins anew.

If these students, teachers, patrons
Had to do my job for a day,
They would not strew their waste
So quickly upon the floor.
I spend my days unrecognized,
Transparent in the crowd
Of acne tortured angst, teenage
Lust and dreams and rage.

I fight the forces of entropy,
Picking up and putting away
The scraps of education that
Don't ever make the grade.
No one aspires for my vocation,
Yet without me they would fail;
The chaos of their passing would
Overwhelm them on their way.

Senioritis

They say that graduation is a commencement,
That the end of something implies a new beginning.
We are mired in that end and time is dragging now.
Why can't the school officials just let us go laughing,
Cutting classes, telling stories, having fun?

What benefit will formal education
Have in these last few weeks
When our time here is essentially all but done?
What can we learn that we don't already know,
Except some arcane and archaic knowledge
That the instructors punish us with learning?

Unlock the doors, unleash the seniors, let us flee free!
Arise, Moses, to our aid, sing "Let my people go."
Stop the homework, discard final exams,
And let us dance before the future
In celebration of that which has been done.
We have served our time, learned our lessons well;
Now let us experience the grace of departure,
The lessons of letting go.

Altered Circumstance

Driving my car home after school,
Traveling swiftly down the road,
Radio blasting, vehicle running smooth,
Thinking of the future, making plans along the way.
I didn't see the other car—
Maybe they didn't see me—
Until it was too late to avoid the crash.
The sound of metal crushing metal
Will haunt my best dreams always.

Now I'm back in school again,
Struggling to walk the way I did
Before circumstance altered my path.
Recovery may be the key concept here,
But I will never travel that road again
Without feeling the fear of fate,
Without sensing the absolute finality of change.

Dumb and Dumber Dudes

Like, in the movies, you know,
They get drunk and party, yeah,
Like, and they get through it OK,
So school should be like, a good time, right?

Parties and bling-bling, you know,
Smokes and tokes, coke and jokes,
We're out for a good time, you know,
Why all this focus on the future stuff?

Live for the moment and party, party, dudes!
Like, what else is there in life?
We don't buy into that goody goody crap;
We're like, really cool, so let's get it on!

We Want Discreet Foreigners!

Do you see that foreign exchange student,
The one with the funny looking face?
Yea, that's him, the gook from a foreign land.
His host family caught him jacking off in the dining room,
Right there above the glass topped table.
He's been downloading too many porno sites,
Must think he's living at Beastie.com.

Why do they let perverts like him over here?
Don't we have enough problems in our own school
Without letting in the scum of others?
What's this country coming too?
I'd never be caught dead doing what he did!
Nope, they'd never catch me–I'd be more discreet!

Awards Assembly

We gather at the end of term
To honor the achievers,
Those students who have raised the bar
Of academic excellence.

Some are athletes, some musicians,
While some are rarely ever seen
Outside the realm of class—
Each, however, has made the grade,
Standouts in the school group.

It's not easy to excel,
To rise above the pressures
Exerted by the mass of peers
Jealous of accomplishment.

To those of you who have achieved,
We award you with high honors—
Certificates of recognition, scholarships and cash—
Tributes to the will and drive
Which marks a student scholar.

Scholarship

Finally it has all paid off!
The hours spent in polishing
Essays of application,
Filling out the many forms,
Studying, hoping, working—
All that effort represented here
By this certificate of award.

There were times when I really wondered
If the chance would materialize
To pursue my education
At the college of my choice.
All those nights of studying,
Passing up the party scene,
Have given me the opportunity
To win this carpe diem day.

With all my heart I thank you,
You fulfillers of this dream,
For faith in me, a student
Who holds the future in my hands.

Either/Or

My sister and I live with my father,
But my mother wants us back.
She's moving again; we go with her, she says,
Or we lose her out of our lives.
She probably really loves us;
It's just that she can't make up her mind
About a husband, a job, a place to call home,
A sunny spot to put down roots.

Dad is doing his best, I suppose,
With his rules and strict discipline.
He wants to protect us, be a real father,
Make up for the years when he wasn't around.
But he was drunk when he picked us up last week
From a weekend at his ex's.
How come he's so hard on us and so easy on himself?

We sisters are torn between two parents—
At least they both want us, unlike some of our friends
Who don't even have a choice.
We make lists of pros and cons
Of living with either/or,
And struggle with issues that shouldn't be issues
If we had a mother who could live with our dad.

Morning Scars

It shouldn't have been a big deal—
She was washing her face in the bathroom
Where her brother usually takes his shower
In the early morning rush that happens before school.

Mean words flew between them
That hurt my heart to hear,
And rage flared up on all sides,
Fanning flames of cruelty.

Tears spilled out of wretched sobs,
Globs of hate bounced bitterly;
The sweetness of the early morn
Turned sour in a few seconds time.

The teenage siblings have forgotten
What they said and did and screamed,
Yet the scars are rough upon my heart;
The wound is bleeding still.

The worst of what I am and was
Is reflected in those acts,
A harvest of hatred reaped from seeds
Planted oh, so long ago.

Is this my legacy in life,
To witness blood on family ties?
I moan a dirge of sad regret
As I hide my soul and weep.

Keynote Speaker

I am the keynote speaker at a conference for kids,
Teenage students who want to help each other find
　　success in life;
The room is full, it is time to commence;
A powerful beginning is the key.

Music opens buds to bloom, unlocks the teenage
　　mind
To receive the message I have to offer:
Love yourself, respect your neighbor,
Learn to be a true friend.

Humor always seems to work—I use different voices
To tell a tale from various views;
I build up confidence and esteem for self while
　　probing
Sensitive places where young people tend to hide.

I expose the fears of their teenage peers—
(Is the water glass half empty or half full?)
Build the connections which make us human
No matter what age/race/color/creed.

I use the stories we all know to draw a pointed
　　moral—
Fairy tales with modern settings;
Keep it moving, keep it real,
Keep it hitting right above the belt.

Merry-go-rounds and adrenalin—these are natural rushes
Some seek through drugs to imitate, but rarely really find.
I parody the experience, get 'em laughing in the aisles,
Fill 'em up with endorphins, promote laughter, the best high.

If I can hold my audience in hand,
Keep these teens from getting bored,
Then I have brought them to the treasure chest.
The message stays the same no matter how it's delivered;

I entertain to educate—that's what makes me special.
The key is getting them to listen.

Holiday Blues

I hate the holidays–
Do I stay with my father,
Or do I go to see my mother?
Both say that they want me there,
But I'm never really sure.
I wasn't enough to hold them
In the family we had formed;
They fought and bickered, finally divorced,
Bounced me in between.
My heart is torn like my love is split;
They struggle over who gets me
Like two hyenas over a chunk of meat,
Flesh formed from their separate souls.
I hate them both! I love them both!
I'd rather be in school.

Lost Spirit

That's my son on the sidelines there,
The one who stands so skinny and small;
His uniform's clean because he hasn't been in—
He'd like a chance to play, that's all.

But the coaches have their favorites
And my son's not among the best
Although he works hard in practices,
Does the workouts with the rest.

All he wants is a chance to show
That he can get the job done—
But the call never comes to put him in—
And for him, watching isn't much fun.

When did we switch from activity for all
To "Win at any cost!!"?
What matters most is not the score;
It's the spirit which is lost.

Anachronism

The future isn't what it used to be,
So said a man of vision long ago.
The seeds of change have taken root
In the compost of the past;
The future's in the womb.

The past is all behind him
Though he won't believe it gone;
In spite of friends and family,
He's ended up alone.

Echoes of the ancient mind–
Dull words upon a page–
The thoughts and lives of yesteryear,
If not brought to life again,
Go unheeded by the young.

Ways change as seasons pass;
Shadows steal the seeing eye.
A rising sun dims the brightest star,
Full moon fades in morning sky.

His is an anachronistic knowledge,
Truths that transcend time.
But the market will not bear it;
Few listen to the old songs.
The great conversation falters.

The tomb stares silent, cold, still;
No thoughts spring from the dead.
But written records of great thoughts
Exist outside cold beds.

Even though the future isn't
What he had in mind,
He still has to breathe
In the here and now
Or life gets left behind.

Evolution versus Creationism

Gnats are nasty selfish bugs
Which swarm and crawl around the face,
Biting with their bitty jaws, earning
Imprecations for their race.

West wind blows without man's grace—
Birds sing under blue/gray skies;
Grass grows tall in the summertime—
The gift of life is a hard won prize.

The results of these our days, it seems,
Is to share our space with other forms
Which compete with us to reproduce,
Find food and shelter from life's storms.

Now some speak truth and some tell lies—
But have gnats evolved from God's own plan?
They give no thought to what they do,
Merely feed upon this thing called man.

What great intelligence would design
A bug without redeeming value?
Unless, of course, the creator works
On a level transcending gnats and you.

Ivory Tower Irony

Just back from a conference at the university
Where a visiting prof with multiple degrees
And a multitude of academic credentials
Harangued his audience on the absolute need
For opening a dialogue between teacher and class.
He lectured incessantly for almost an hour
On the evils of the mono logical presentation—
And in the end ran out of time
For questions and responses from the audience.

Why I am a Teacher

There are many complex reasons for why I teach;
Sit down and chat if you have a while;
We'll discuss educational philosophies,
Altruism, and instructional styles.
Time is of the essence always;
Good teachers work hard at what they do.
And if you think educators have it made,
Well, the door is open—walk on through.

But before you pass judgment on this profession,
Ask yourself a thing or two—
Do you have the personality required,
The skills to shape a mind anew?
Are you an organized interactor?
Can you plan, direct, and guide?
Can you engage diverse groups of kids
As they carom through their adolescent ride?

Do you have patience, empathy, and a smile?
Can you challenge a student reluctant to learn?
Can you set high standards and expect the best,
And from this thorny path not turn?
If you can complete the college course work,
Pass tests, write papers, talk the talk,
Next spend some time in the classroom—
Try practice teaching—walk the walk!

Then put some years in refining techniques;
Immerse yourself fully in the fire.
Perform the myriad duties and tasks
They never mention when you are hired.
If you've the energy to do all of this,
Plus sponsor extracurricular events on the side,
Then maybe education is really for you—
Maybe a calling in your heart resides.

But if you really don't have the time or desire,
And you still wonder why I'm a teacher,
Let me make it simple for you;
I'll explain an alluring feature.
Upon my hand five fingers stand;
Each point is a student celebration;
Make a fist: Spring Break, June, July,
August, and Christmas Vacation!

Semester's End

Another class has passed on through;
They know more now than what they knew,
But so many things they didn't do—
True learning touches but a few.

As a teacher I have tried
To show them what they need inside
Their minds and hearts to be a guide
Upon life's sometimes stormy ride.

Now they're leaving out the door—
Lessons for me they'll write no more;
But hopefully they've learned a core
Of knowledge they will need before

They can build a stable base
For encountering the human race.